Captain Courage

D1099590

FROM STOCK

4721800003646 0

Captain Courage

Gareth Thomas

Published by Accent Press Ltd 2015

ISBN 9781783759132

Copyright © **Gareth Thomas** 2015

The right of **Gareth Thomas** to be identified as the author of this work has been asserted by the author in accordance with the Copyright, Designs and Patents Act 1988.

All rights reserved. No part of this book may be reproduced, stored in a retrieval system, or transmitted in any form or by any means, electronic, electrostatic, magnetic tape, mechanical, photocopying, recording or otherwise, without the written permission of the publishers: Accent Press Ltd, Ty Cynon House, Navigation Park, Abercynon, CF45 4SN

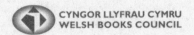

CYNGOR LLYFRAU CYMRU
WELSH BOOKS COUNCIL

Noddir gan
Lywodraeth Cymru
Sponsored by
Welsh Government

Chapter 1

'Gareth Thomas is a hundred percenter! He always gave a hundred per cent both in training and on match day.'
Jonathan Davies MBE, Wales and British and Irish Lions, Great Britain rugby league international

My first memory of rugby was the joy of just running with the ball in Bryncethin Junior School near Bridgend. It was fun and there was no pressure. But when I joined the comprehensive school, things were different. The school was so much bigger and you actually had to show you could play the game before you got into the team. For my first session, my mother had bought me rugby boots from Woolworths. Everybody else had Adidas or Nike rugby boots! I felt as if everyone was thinking, 'Well, he's not going to be any good with rugby boots from Woolworths!'

However, I remember being quite good in training and learnt quickly that it's the quality of the person that matters, not the boots. I realised at a very young age how much I loved rugby and what the game of rugby meant to me. I enjoyed being part of a team and understood that while we were all different, we all had something to offer. For me, the game was about sharing skills and not about being a star because you were the speediest or the strongest on the pitch. I was always fast in school but I wasn't someone who was picked out as being special. Even though I loved the game, I was far from being the outstanding player in the team. I wasn't the one who could change the course of a game or do magic things to win a match. I wasn't even close to that. If I was selected to play, to me that seemed a massive achievement as I never felt I excelled as others did. I was picked as a substitute a lot of the time, and I was happy with that as it still gave me a role to play. Others might react badly to being put on the bench and have a strop or a sulk about it, but it never bothered me. I told myself that the team was what mattered.

My PE teacher at Ogmore School, Mr John, was my inspiration. Years later, I was touched to learn that he turned up regularly to watch me play for Bridgend but never made himself known to me. PE and Mr John were the only reasons I went to school. To know that he had seen me doing really well was very special to me. He was a typical sports teacher, willing to give hours and hours outside of school during the week and on Saturday mornings so that his teams did well. He was strict, with very clear boundaries for what he would and wouldn't accept from us on and off the pitch. He understood the boys who needed sport in school to let off steam. He made going to school bearable for me. He gave me a reason to go to classes. I don't think I would have gone if he hadn't been there. I would sit through eight lessons a day to be able to do one lesson of PE!

English was one other subject I liked. I was quite creative and I enjoyed reading plays but as a 'sporty' boy that didn't really fit in with my image. Everything else failed to inspire me so I was happy to leave school at sixteen. I knew I was never going to get A grades and that gave me the drive and ambition to go for the one thing I was good at – rugby. My parents knew that too and could see there was no point in forcing me to stay in school. I started my GCSE exams but I didn't want to complete them. It was horrible sitting an exam with very little to write, while everyone around me seemed to be filling in page after page. Lessons, exams and school were not for me.

My parents made it clear that I could leave, but only once I had found myself a job. So I went to the Job Centre with my mum the very day that I finished my exams and saw a job advertised in a local factory. The next day I started in Pressrite Engineering in Bridgend, making filters. It was the hardest job I have ever had in my life. I remember, at the end of that first day of work, I came home at five o'clock and said to my mother that I wanted to go upstairs for an hour before tea. I was absolutely shattered, went to bed and woke up the next morning still in my working clothes. I couldn't believe it. This was what real work was like!

I stayed at Pressrite Engineering for six or seven months until my father got me an apprenticeship as a postman like him. I moved up to earning £125 a week, which was a fortune to me! I really enjoyed working as a postman. I was becoming quite good at rugby by now and the job became like an extra sports session for me. I'd go on my round, carrying really heavy bags of letters and parcels and run the round as if I was training. I'd go to the gym straight afterwards and then go back to the post office for the second deliveries and run the routes again. After work, I'd go home, have a short sleep, and get up and go training at Pencoed Rugby Club in the evening. It was hard but it made me fit. I liked meeting people on my rounds and being out in the open air in my town, a place that meant the world to me.

I had the best time at Pencoed Rugby Club. It had a close-knit friendly community atmosphere and everyone looked out for one another. I learned my trade at the club.

This was proper rugby. The sign outside the club said it all for me: 'Pencoed Rugby Club – Delivering community rugby at its best'. I felt comfortable there and one of the boys when we chanted our team song:

'Who are... Who are... Who are we?
We are Pencoed RFC.
We don't swear. We don't fight.
We're the boys in red, blue, white.'

This was my world. I just loved being with my mates and putting all my energies into a sport that was my life.

I played for Pencoed until Bridgend signed me. I was thrilled when they did. Now I was able to play for a great club with a great rugby tradition. Players like J.P.R. Williams, J.J. Williams and Steve Fenwick had attracted huge crowds to the Brewery Field and had gone on to play for Wales and the British and Irish Lions. People used to say to my parents that I, too, was going to be a great player in the future and that they could see me playing for my country. It was nice to hear that but I was always more proud of compliments I got from people I played with. I looked up to more established players like Glen Webbe, the former Wales winger, and when he praised me it felt important and really meant something. I didn't get carried away, but it was encouraging.

This was a very happy time in my life. I was still a postman, even when I was playing for Bridgend. I was playing for the town where I had grown up and I was thrilled to be representing a place that I loved. In the week, I'd be out walking the streets and chatting to people who on a Saturday would be coming to watch me play rugby. I felt proud to be part of this community. I was their postman and their player and, to me, it was so much more than just a game of rugby. Rugby was the life and very soul of the town and when we beat the bigger clubs like

Cardiff, Swansea or Neath it was brilliant, because it put Bridgend on top. I never genuinely thought I would play for Wales. I was just happy to have what I had always wanted, a life in sport. Lots of people along the way told me I had potential and said that, one day, I would play for my country. But I just thought people were being nice and I never took them seriously.

One day, Glen Webbe bet me a hundred pounds, a fortune to me then, that in the future I would play for Wales. I just laughed, but in 1995 I was selected for the Welsh squad to go to South Africa for the World Cup. The day I played for Wales he sent me a telegram saying, 'You owe me a hundred pounds.' He'd been right! The first thing I did when I got home from the tour was to go to see him and pay up on the bet. It was the best hundred pounds I ever paid out!

Chapter 2

*'Gareth was a young inexperienced tourist at the
1995 World Cup but I recognised that he had the
potential to be one of Wales' greatest players and he
has achieved that honour.'*
Robert Jones MBE, Wales and British and Irish Lions

One day my father collected the mail for our house at the sorting office to save the postman a delivery and he couldn't believe it when, in the middle of the parcels and bills, he saw a letter addressed to me with the magic letters WRU on the back of the envelope. I was sorting out my own post round and he raced straight over to where I was working. He stood next to me, waving the letter in excitement, saying, 'There's a letter from the Welsh Rugby Union!'

He wouldn't move from my side, waiting for me to tell him what was inside. I opened the letter and stared at it, unable quite to believe what was in front of me. I had been invited to join the squad training to go to the World Cup in South Africa in 1995. My father was so happy that I was being asked to join the huge Wales squad. I will never forget his face and how proud he was for me. My parents are the world to me and I was so glad that he was part of such a key moment in my life. I have always looked up to my parents and this moment was even more special because I knew what it meant to them, too.

I went to the World Cup, never expecting to play, but

going there to train hard and to learn. The day before the team was announced, Steve Ford, the ex-winger from Cardiff, came up and congratulated me. I was confused until he told me that he wouldn't be playing and, therefore, I must have been chosen to play on the wing. I didn't believe him and thought that someone else was sure to be picked. I never thought it was possible that I might be on the list. When they announced the team the next day and my name was there, it was like a dream come true.

The jerseys were presented to us in the changing room the day before the game and I remember not knowing what to do with mine, as it was so precious. I'd heard stories of players who slept in their jerseys or who put them under their pillows all night. I had to think what would be best to inspire me and not just rely on what worked for others. So I hung my Welsh jersey in the most prominent place in my room where I could gaze at it all night. Then I took huge pride in putting it on, conscious of the three feathers placed over my heart. I filled up with pride and the determination to give my all. Just touching the badge of honour for my country inspired me. I thought proudly of all the players who had worn the Welsh jersey before me and what they must have been thinking as they received their shirts for the first time. This time, the honour was mine. It was up to me to do my best as other Welshmen had. Now that I had it in my possession, I had to do it justice and hold on it for as long as I could.

The pre-match speeches were very special and memorable to me. I listened carefully to the words of older, more experienced players and respected their thoughts on what it was like to win that first jersey and the advice they had chosen especially for that moment.

The first game I played for Wales, in a green jersey, was

in the World Cup against Japan in the Free State Stadium in Bloemfontein, South Africa. I was one of two new caps that day, the other being Andy Moore, the Cardiff scrum half. It was an amazing debut for me as I scored a hat trick of tries and Wales won 57–10. Even then, I refused to take it all in and just kept telling myself that I had to keep working hard. I couldn't get carried away as the day wasn't about what I did, but about what the team achieved.

I remember hardly anything about the game as it all passed in a blur. People tell you to hold the moment but it all goes so quickly. I remember being proud to be part of a squad with greats like Mike Hall, Stuart Davies, Garin Jenkins and Robert Jones. These were the legends of Welsh rugby to me, the people I looked up to and wanted to be like. Throughout the tour I roomed with Robert, a most talented and highly-respected scrum half, and learnt so much from the way he coped under pressure. I wanted to be like that. He must have realised how naïve I was – I still talked about Bridgend all the time! But he and I got on really well because he took me under his wing. He showed me the ropes and helped me deal with fans and journalists. The whole tour was a whirlwind for me and, even though I was desperate to remember every detail, everything went by too quickly. I began to realise that these rugby heroes, my fellow teammates, were real people and not just stars who were cheered every match day. We were all proud to play our part and work together for each other and for Wales. We all understood what being selected to play for Wales meant and the responsibility we had to those who travelled far and wide to support us.

My next game was against New Zealand and I partnered Mike Hall in the centre, playing against the iconic Frank

Bunce and Walter Little, considered by many to be one of the finest centre pairings ever to have played in the famous black jersey with the silver fern. I was nineteen years of age, scrawny, tall and up against the huge All Blacks team. Ellis Park in Johannesburg was the biggest stadium I had ever seen, able to hold sixty-thousand spectators, and it seemed as if each one of them was screaming at full voice. I looked around, completely in awe of my surroundings. It was humbling to stand in the tunnel side by side great rugby players like the New Zealand captain, Sean Fitzpatrick, and the giant Jonah Lomu, who was being called the sensation of the tournament. I remember thinking, 'What am I doing here? What is going to happen?' I had to keep telling myself that I deserved to be there. I tried hard to forget about the occasion, the atmosphere and the ground and to imagine that I was where I was happiest – the boy from Bridgend playing rugby on the Brewery Field. How lucky was I to have this chance to play against the best players in the world!

I learned so much that day. Even though we lost, it was one of the few times that Jonah Lomu failed to score – which was a source of great pride to me and my teammates. Just to be on the same field as the All Blacks was a great opportunity and I gave the game everything I had.

People ask what the haka can do to you before a big game. They ask: do you feel scared? Or do you try to front it up? And what do you think about? I can't remember facing the haka that day. I simply waited, lining up with the other Welsh players to accept the challenge. I could only concentrate on what was about to take place and keep my focus on what I had to do for the team. I was there ready to play for my country in the Welsh team. Despite the fearsome haka challenge of the All Blacks, I didn't worry about the star-studded team we were facing – it was the pride and passion of playing for Wales that inspired me in those last few minutes before kick-off. We started strongly and confidently and the Welsh flags were raised around the stadium, but this was a different match from my debut. We lost 34–9 against a much better team.

The next game, against Ireland, was a terrible one for us. We had to win to stay in the competition. I played on the wing that day but it was a game of rugby that never started. The team couldn't settle at all. The stadium was packed with Welsh and Irish supporters singing and cheering loudly. Celtic songs filled the stadium and 'Fields of Athenry' and 'Calon Lân' were sung with gusto and fervour to urge on the teams. Wales won the toss, but after that I can't remember touching the ball and I learned that things can change quickly and don't always go the way you want them to go. We lost by just one point, 24–23. Not to reach the quarterfinals was a huge disappointment for everyone. After the game, everyone was quiet. It was painful not to achieve the things we had trained so hard for and set out to do. The eighty minutes were over and we were out. The team atmosphere was dark and depressing. We were all aware of how much this meant to the Welsh fans who, like us, had travelled to South Africa with high expectations of getting through the group, at the very least. Everyone felt down as we returned home without the victory we had hoped for. For us, the dream of the World Cup was over.

Chapter 3

'I christened him Gareth, not Alfie!'
Yvonne Thomas (Gareth's mum)

I was never superstitious about the game. Some players needed to put their right sock on before their left one or leave their jersey hanging up until the very last minute. Some players had to whistle before going to the tunnel, while others had to make sure their kit was laid out in the same way in the changing room every time. If these things didn't happen, it could affect their performance before the game had even started. I didn't want to be part of that. It would have been too easy to blame outside factors. I just liked to stay focused on what was in front of me. In the changing room, I liked to chat with others about something other than the game. When I was younger it was easy to become vulnerable to things that would distract me, so I liked to keep on track by talking to the more experienced players. I wanted to remember who I was and where I was.

Walking through the tunnel onto the pitch in front of a crowd of seventy thousand people, not only could I hear the atmosphere in the stadium, but I could actually feel it too! Before a game, little by little, the singing and chanting would build into a wall of powerful sound. By the time I ran out with my teammates to represent our country you couldn't hear yourself think. This was my time: the time I loved the best. I had to keep it together. I couldn't let the emotion take over or I would lose my clear thinking, my 'rugby mind'. It was impossible not to be nervous but I understood it was good to have that feeling to keep myself sharp. However, I always wanted to be in control of my nervous energy and my excitement. In rugby, although the format is very familiar – same rules, two teams, eighty minutes, an oval ball and a referee – each game is unique. Preparation and pre-match speeches can take you so far, but the important time is when the whistle goes to start the match. That's when the adrenalin flowed and I was ready to take on the best.

On my return from the World Cup, I signed my first professional contract for £18,000 a year with Bridgend. As an amateur player I had been used to ten pounds in an envelope at the end of each game, so this was an amazing amount to me. I was offered much more money to sign for Salford or Bradford and play rugby league but I declined – at heart I was still the boy from Bridgend. The first time my parents came to see me play for Wales was in 1996, in what was then the Five Nations rugby championship. Sadly we didn't shine, beating only France that year to avoid a whitewash in the championship. It was not the result I wanted my parents to witness. I wanted them to see that their sacrifices and support for me had all been worth it.

I knew my parents had worked long hours to get kit for me when I needed it over the years. Also, there was all the additional 'driving work' like every rugby parent, taking me backwards and forwards to training and to all the different grounds for matches. I'm the youngest of three boys and my brothers, Steven and Richard, always said I was the spoilt one. Their nickname for me was, and still is, 'Goldenballs'!

My parents say that I certainly had the most energy!

Every Saturday, they would drive the three of us to different games, watch twenty minutes of each of us playing, perhaps at entirely different ends of the valley, and then do the whole trip all over again to collect us at the end. As a child I thought travelling was free. I didn't think of the cost of petrol and all the extra time that they gave so willingly to us. My parents made huge sacrifices for us all and I can never thank them enough. They never said it was a sacrifice but, looking back, I can see how much they gave up for us to have the necessary equipment. We were three sport-mad boys and we all liked different sports. I loved tennis and karate. I had all the kit for each so it was a lot of money for my parents to find. They have said that there wasn't a sport on the planet I didn't try! But they encouraged us to play sport because they believed that learning to abide by rules and regulations was an important lesson for us to learn. They saw how vital it was for us to appreciate success and failure. Those were values we also learned from them at home. The lessons of rugby were hard ones but, as I grew up, I realised that along with glory there came pressure too.

The pressures of playing rugby changed when it became a professional sport. Kevin Bowring, the new Welsh coach, and the team were now being paid and the public expected value for money. Yet Wales was no longer the great rugby force it used to be and the public and the press told us so in no uncertain terms. Everyone had an opinion and wasn't afraid to share it. Alfie – my old school nickname – had become public property. I'd been named after Alf, Alien Life Form, from the American children's TV programme, and mention of me in the newspaper headlines was usually followed with tales of my wild behaviour both on the pitch and off. The character's misadventures seemed to be just like mine – though I stopped short of trying to eat the family cat! I was known as a joker by some, the new Welsh rugby saviour to others, and a complete liability to the rest. My mother didn't appreciate my 'new' name and made her feelings known. She complained, 'I christened him Gareth, not Alfie!' but the name stuck and soon everyone seemed to use it.

The public Alfie and the private Gareth started to become further and further apart. I needed to go back to the values I had been brought up to believe in. Alfie was the powerful hard man of rugby, forceful and dominant on the pitch. I presented myself as macho by being deliberately on the offensive. But I was getting out of control and alcohol only made me worse. I used confrontation and anger to keep people from recognising a secret that was tearing me apart. This secret was that I was gay. Two of my closest friends had guessed and tried to offer me a chance to talk, but I was too scared and could see all my hopes and dreams exploding if I told the truth. I didn't expect people to understand and I hit out verbally at those who tried to support me. I feel ashamed as I look back at how I behaved with those who were generous in never giving up on me. I lived in fear of being caught out. I saw myself as public property, a rugby player known by all of Wales, and therefore always liable to be held to account.

In 1998, Wales lost to England 60–26, France 51–0 and South Africa 96–13. Kevin Bowring's reign as coach was over. The New Zealander Graham Henry, 'The Great Redeemer', replaced him on a five-year contract worth £1.25 million. I, too, made a change, moving from my beloved Bridgend to play for Cardiff. I had to move to play at the highest level to improve my international game but it was a difficult decision and I was thankful to those who understood and wished me well. Not everyone did but that was to be expected, given the powerful club loyalties in rugby. In a professional world, money was also a factor.

People knew my name now and the pressure grew on me to conform to the life that all my teammates had. I had been going out with Jemma, my teenage sweetheart, for a long time and got married to her in 2001 in St Bridget's Church just outside Bridgend. I saw this as a statement that I would settle down and become the person I hoped I could be, a family man. Sadly, Wales lost 15–44 to England in that year and I was losing control and living a lie. I enjoyed drinking and mad nights out. I cheated on Jemma with faceless flings in London, unable to admit to myself that at home I was trying to be someone I was not. As hard as I tried, I was unable to settle. I had hoped desperately to be the husband Jemma deserved and felt appalled that I wasn't. I felt sickened by my lies and the change in me. I hoped things would get better when I returned to play for Bridgend in 2001.

In 2002, I had been relegated to the second string, now disbanded, Wales 'A' team. In what was to be Graham Henry's last game as manager of Wales, I had to watch from the sidelines as Ireland defeated us 54–10. I was no longer the schoolboy who believed that it was all about the team and was prepared to sit it out until chosen. I felt angry and resentful that I was not selected. My attitude did not go unnoticed by the new manager, Steve Hansen. He and I didn't like each other at first. When he dropped me from the Welsh squad completely it was a dreadful blow to me. His words hit hard. He told me that I had played numerous times for Wales but that I showed no more seniority in a meeting or on the training field than a brand new player. He felt I was happy to be popular but offered no more than that. He didn't feel I gave enough and he saw that as a lack of respect for the team and for the talent I had been given.

These were hard words to hear. He dropped me from the squad for a couple of weeks so that I would appreciate the honour of playing for my country. He told me that the only way I would learn was by not being part of the squad. Steve told me this straight. I felt humiliated but knew why he had said what he had and in my heart realised that things had to change. I had to understand again what playing for Wales and representing my country meant to me. I have a great deal to thank Steve Hansen for. He reinvented the player who would then go on to gain one hundred caps for his country. It wouldn't have happened without his intervention and I'll always be grateful to him.

Chapter 4

'Alfie was an ideal role model for young, aspiring professional rugby players. He was a superb athlete, dedicated and totally committed to Bridgend and Wales. Even though he enjoyed superstar status, as captain of Bridgend, he always made a real effort to listen to and represent the views of all of the squad members – senior and junior players alike. Indeed, he was a man "who walked with kings but never lost the common touch". He was a good man.'

Allan Lewis, Bridgend coach

I returned to play for Bridgend where coach Allan Lewis decided to make me captain. I was able to concentrate on playing well for Bridgend, as I was no longer away with the Wales rugby team as much. I began to realise how much I enjoyed the role of leader and how much more serious and responsible I could be when I did the job properly. Allan's reputation and experience in the world of rugby was well known and I needed to learn from him. He understood the game and, more importantly, he understood players. His skills and experience in coaching allowed me to develop. I started to play well and enjoy the game as I had before. Thanks to his guidance, I got back into the Welsh team and impressed Steve Hansen with a new attitude and determination. Steve had been right to force me to look hard at myself and prove that I was not wasting the gift that had been given to me.

I had grown up as a player and, more importantly, as a leader, which was what both coaches had been aiming for. By offering me the captaincy of Wales, against Ireland in Dublin in 2003, Steve was acknowledging that I was now ready to start achieving my potential for my country, my team and myself. He told me that he was impressed with the way that I had listened to his words and come back. He wanted me to guide the team and take control. This was a huge challenge for me but he told me not to be afraid. He inspired me to believe that I was ready and capable of doing the job. I felt honoured by that. This was the culmination of a lot of hard work with Bridgend and I wanted to show that I was worthy of his faith in me.

I also saw it as an important test for myself, at the highest level. I felt the responsibility of the role. Rugby affects the mood of the Welsh people. When Wales win, people are happy. For many, rugby is central to their life and as a player and a captain, playing the game at the highest level, I understood that. Once again, I loved every minute of it and did everything I could to improve and help others. I needed to show that I had grown as a player and as a leader. Some of the press coverage was not positive, but that only spurred me to show the media that I wanted to do the role well. I was the last person the public expected to be offered the role of captain. Many talked about what a huge risk it was to offer me this important role. I was determined to prove the doubters wrong and to show those who believed in me that they were right to have done so.

From day one as Welsh captain, I recognised that I couldn't just expect people to follow me straight away. I knew it would take time and that I would have to earn the respect of the players.

To guide and control a changing room of sports people

full of emotions is a very special skill. The players were the best in Wales, and some of the best in the world and I recognised that. They had to believe in me and trust me as their captain. And I had to lead from the front. This was a new start for me. Before, I would have been afraid to try, but my new-found attitude told me to be excited, not afraid, of the challenge. It was a chance to show them what I was prepared to do.

There were also new skills I needed to take on. I had to learn to 'read' a changing room, to understand what makes people react in different ways and what makes them tick. I needed to get to know people and they needed to get to know me. Some players need absolute silence before a game and can't talk to anyone. Others want to talk and need to let their emotions loose. Some need loud music or messages to motivate them. Others need to be alone. By learning all these things, I was learning more about myself, too. I told myself that I had to do this key job properly and I threw myself into the role, determined to give everything I had to show I was worthy of the honour.

In 2003, I was proud to captain Bridgend to a Welsh Premier Division title where we were unbeaten at home and lost only to Cardiff and Neath, away. Things were improving for me, it seemed. I trained harder than my teammates, determined to show them not only my dedication, but also as a smokescreen to hide any thoughts of my sexuality, which I saw as a weakness that could catch me out. I needed to be a beast of a man on the field. I wanted to prove that I excelled at rugby and was a 'rugby man' – everything that society seemed to say that gay men couldn't be.

Then, just before the 2003–4 season began, there came a severe test for us all – the introduction of five regional teams in Wales. This marked the start of a tough revolutionary period in Welsh rugby history. When Bridgend amalgamated with Pontypridd it was a terrible time for players, coaches and fans. We knew that people would lose their jobs and two proud distinct rugby teams would be destroyed to create one new team, the Celtic Warriors. After one season as their captain, we were shut down. I tried my best to make sure that every person had somewhere to go by representing them in meetings about their future. I was concerned that all of the players were well cared for. I felt it was my duty as captain to do the right thing by the guys who had followed me on the field. Players had to go the length and breadth of the country looking for other clubs. I felt completely down-hearted and no longer wanted to be part of a system that had treated people in this way.

However, I was fortunate enough to be approached to join the iconic French rugby team Toulouse. I was signed to replace the outstanding Emile Ntamack – so no pressure! It is not an exaggeration to call Toulouse the Real Madrid of rugby. The club is traditionally one of the main providers of players to the French national team. They are one of the finest rugby clubs in Europe with a serious supporter base. The red and black colours, 'rouge et noir' as the team are known, proudly and distinctly show off a club where rugby culture and skills are highly valued. I saw the move as good for me in terms of rugby and also for a change of lifestyle. The contract was £285,000 a year and there were sponsorship deals too. This was the big time as far as I was concerned!

When I moved to France, it was hard being out of my comfort zone. Simple things that I took for granted were suddenly difficult for me. I remember going out for milk for my breakfast and realising in the shop that I had no idea how to ask for it! I had to smile and point and make signs, and I could see how hard I would need to work to fit into a life in a different country. I didn't need to learn the language for the club, as everyone spoke English, but I needed to show them I wanted to fit in. I wanted to be part of this successful set-up and for them to know I was making an effort.

I had French lessons but I found that difficult as it brought back awful memories of school! Instead, I started watching DVDs of films I had already seen at home, but this time, watched them in French to pick up words and phrases. As the French players always wanted to practise their English, I asked them to speak to me in English, and then I would try to speak a few words to them in French. I felt it was important that I showed them respect and by trying to learn and use a few words of French I earned a lot of praise. At first, just like at school, I was afraid to open my mouth and try because I was scared of failing. The French players showed me that they preferred to see me try and not to get it quite right than not try at all. It was a good lesson to learn!

As a team we would breakfast together, then train together, eat a large lunch, then go home for a couple of hours and maybe chill out by the pool. We would train again in the evening. It was a different lifestyle and culture from the one I had left back home but I understood why it worked. I thrived on it and enjoyed every minute.

Toulouse, in Midi-Pyrénées, opened my eyes to new experiences. I had joined an elite list of names like a 'who's who' of rugby – Frédéric Michalak, Yannick Jauzion, Vincent Clerc, Fabien Pelous, Thierry Dusautoir, Trevor Brennan and Cédric Heymans. All stars in their own right. I learned a great deal in my four years at the club and was always keen to give them my best. We were the team that everyone wanted to beat. Teams that came to play us thought that because we were such a galaxy of stars we would not be a tight unit, looking out for each other. They couldn't have been more wrong. They tried to target us as individuals, but we were bonded and team spirit was central to our training. I loved the coaching culture in training, which was to play what you saw in front of you and be instinctive. In Stade Toulousain, training was really physical and we were given actual scenarios that we might have to react to during a game. I came from a more structured system in Wales and playing like this allowed me to try things I had never tried before.

I soon became aware of how important the players were to the city of Toulouse. Now I understood how a Manchester United or Real Madrid star must feel as I walked around. Heads turned as I passed and people smiled and pointed at me. We were treated like gods in a city where rugby is like religion. It was a special honour to be signed as a foreign player in a team where they pride themselves on choosing French players wherever possible. Just imagine how I felt as part of the Toulouse team that won the Heineken Cup!

Chapter 5

'Whenever I faced Gareth, in any team he was captain of, you knew you had to be prepared to go that extra ruck, that extra tackle, that extra sprint as he committed everything to the game, the team and to the win. He left everything on the pitch and you had to be prepared to suffer and sacrifice more. As soon as he walked off that pitch, he became the lovable Gareth we all know. That's what I liked about him.'

Phil Greening, England international

In 2004 I was made captain of Wales again after attending a formal interview with Mike Ruddock, who had taken over from Steve Hansen as coach. This was a completely new experience for me. I applied for the captaincy and it was a tough call for me to go through an interview process. I can remember knocking on the door, full of nerves, and formally introducing myself to the selection panel. It was certainly a different process to be chosen like this, but it proved very successful. I realise now that having to apply in this way, rather than being selected, forced me to show how much I wanted to be the leader.

The Six Nations championship started well with a narrow two-point victory over England, the old enemy, at home. Beating England gave us confidence. It was good to start with a win against the pre-tournament favourites. I walked to the team bus with Martyn Williams ('Nugget' to me), still grinning and wanting to enjoy the victory but also wanting to hold something back. I knew that to relax too early was dangerous. I wanted to wait until all of our matches were over as I felt there was better to come!

After this, three good wins on the road against Italy, France and Scotland set up a mouth-watering final match against Ireland at the Millennium Stadium in Cardiff. The magic of the stadium got to us all. The pre-match singing of 'Delilah' and 'Hymns and Arias' set us up well. The sound of the regimental band reached us in the dressing room and stirred us all as 'Guide me, O thou Great Redeemer' got louder and louder. 'Feed me 'til I want no more' was in our heads and hearts. We stood listening to the anthem, knowing that we were there representing Wales, our country. The passion of the crowd singing was all the encouragement we needed to spur us on.

We beat Ireland, Wales won the Grand Slam and, despite being in a plaster cast after an injury in Paris, I proudly held aloft the trophy with the Welsh captain for the game, Michael Owen. I had wanted Steve Jones, the Newport Gwent Dragons hooker, to collect the cup because he had been an important part of the thirty-man training squad even though he had never actually been selected for a match. I'd wanted to show how much I valued everyone in the entire team and it had seemed fitting to do this. In the end my idea wasn't taken up but it is something I have always felt important. A team stands or falls by every person's contribution and I made sure that the victory celebrations showed that.

The mood in Wales was just like it had been in Toulouse when we won the Heineken Cup – it seemed everyone had come out to celebrate. People were dancing in the streets, ready to name their babies after their favourite players and Cardiff was a sea of red and green with dragons proudly held up high. It was the place to be!

There is nothing like a win at the Millennium Stadium in the capital city. I sat back and drank in the atmosphere, unable to stop grinning with joy at what we had achieved. Cardiff was buzzing and the mood didn't stop after the match. For some time after, I still had people thanking me for being part of the team that had put Welsh rugby back in its rightful position, the best of the six nations! Wales is a small country but, after a win like that, everyone claimed to have been at the stadium that day!

Next on the horizon for me was the British and Irish Lions tour of New Zealand in 2005. Clive Woodward was the coach and his detailed planning was very different from the preparation I was used to. By nature, I am driven by feelings, history and pride, and these things stir me to raise my game. In New Zealand we were facing a team who wanted to win at all costs: that's why the All Blacks are so good. We were defeated in the first Test and our captain Brian O'Driscoll, the legendary Irish outside centre, was injured in the infamous spear tackle incident and was not fit to play in the second Test or for the rest of the tour.

I was made the thirty-fifth captain of the tour. My parents were the first to hear my news. I was saddened for Brian, an honourable and excellent player for whom I had the greatest respect. I wanted to rise to the challenge for the good of the team and for Brian. He was dignified, even though he was in pain and, though he was clearly destroyed that he had to leave the tour, he wished me luck in taking over his role. This captaincy was a very different job for me. It was not just leading my fellow countrymen, but dealing with players from different nations who I had to inspire to pull together for each other and for the good of the team. My plan was to spur everyone on by my actions on the field, rather than by rallying them with a dramatic team talk. In my book, actions spoke louder than words.

It didn't work. We lost 48–18 and my post-match behaviour was not the best... The third Test result was no better: we lost 38–19. It was another horrendous defeat and we all knew that the All Blacks motto, 'Subdue and Penetrate', had proved right yet again. Richie McCaw's men were the victors throughout. We quietly left New Zealand to return home.

I learned a lot about myself from this experience of captaining people from different countries and different backgrounds. In sport there are winners and losers, and we couldn't moan about having lost to such a powerful team. The All Blacks were, and are, amazing and we knew we had lost because we weren't as good as them.

One highlight of the Tour for me had been meeting up with Prince William and his bodyguard in Wellington. Even though he is a passionate England fan and is often seen at matches giving them his support, he listened eagerly to the tales from the Welsh pair – myself and Tom Shanklin. Some of our stories were certainly interesting and colourful... but he seemed to take it all in good part.

Even so, in 2011, I was shocked to receive a grand envelope through the post inviting me to the wedding of HRH Prince William, Duke of Cambridge, to Miss Catherine Middleton. The post has so often been good to me! I couldn't believe it. When the day came, I sat in Westminster Abbey, looking around at all the royalty, politicians and famous people drinking in the spectacle of a royal wedding. Outside, London was celebrating wildly. Millions were tuned in to their televisions around the world. Yet, as Max Boyce said, 'I was there!' Guests like

David Cameron, Carwyn Jones and Boris Johnson filed in alongside Richard Branson, Elton John and David and Victoria Beckham. Martyn Williams and I joked with each other that we were members of the Welsh rugby royal family, so we were in good company! I was told that we were both listed under 'Celebrities and other notable guests' on the Internet – that was a story we could dine out on in rugby circles for years to come!

Sadly, I had to turn down an invitation to the evening party given by Sir Elton John as I had to train with the Crusaders in Wrexham, north Wales. I took a lot of stick from my teammates. They were all very interested to hear about the wedding, but the real joy for them was knowing that I had to miss out on a party with amazing food and drink and the chance to rub shoulders with the stars! They all secretly just wanted to be there in my place.

Chapter 6

'He is my best friend and my family's too. What a bloke! Duw gadwo ef.'
Ian 'Compo' Greenslade, former Bridgend captain and
Gareth's trusted friend

Life after the Grand Slam of 2005 sadly did not continue in the same spirit of 'All for one and one for all'. There were problems as in many teams and organisations. Mike Ruddock decided to leave as coach to the Wales team and the rumours were that his decision was due to 'player power', the leading culprit being me as captain. The players had little idea of what was happening and I was being portrayed as the bad guy, and it hurt. Other names were bandied about and the situation became very unpleasant. It was horrible for my friends and family to see me described as 'backstabbing'. The rugby message boards and websites were buzzing with different theories as to what was going on. It is easy for rumours to spread and soon the media were involved and headlines of team conspiracies appeared more and more.

I decided to return from France to appear on *Scrum V*, BBC Wales' flagship rugby programme, and talk for the team. I was convinced it was the only way to defend the players. My parents picked me up from Bristol Airport and tried to talk me out of what they saw as the wrong thing to do. They had seen all the build-up on news programmes as well as sports shows and knew there would be trouble ahead.

I arrived at the studio for the recording expecting a difficult interview, but was in no way prepared for what happened. Gareth Lewis, the *Scrum V* presenter, introduced us with the words, 'From Grand Slam to grand farce – it's been quite a week and it could get even hotter this evening.' He wasn't wrong!

In the debate that followed, I clashed with Eddie Butler, a former captain of Wales and an extremely knowledgeable and clever television commentator and sports journalist. Looking back, I should never have been party to this. I wanted to represent the team as their captain but doing this on screen, without preparing carefully what I wanted to say, was not sensible. I became extremely worked up and challenged Eddie to say what he thought he knew, live on television. 'You tell us on TV!' I said.

Eddie's response was much more calm and measured and he seemed in control of the situation, being much more used to a studio setting. Martyn Williams, the Wales and British Lions flanker, and a trusted friend and teammate, put it best when he said later of me: 'He was up against Eddie Butler, Cambridge Blue and one of the most articulate men you'll ever meet. Alf's from the university of Sarn!' (Sarn is the village outside Bridgend where I was born.)

I lost my cool completely and felt I had to state publicly and loudly: 'Did everyone get that live on telly? I didn't express concerns about his [Mike Ruddock's] coaching!' Jonathan Davies, another former Welsh captain and *Scrum V* main pundit, and presenter Gareth Lewis were open-mouthed. They couldn't believe what they were seeing and hearing. I was in a dreadful state, releasing all the anger and pain that was in my head.

I left the studio with my parents and drove back in silence from the television studios in Llandaff to my home, going over everything again and again. I met up with Jemma and my friends Ian 'Compo' and Catherine, having planned to watch the programme being broadcast. But I began to feel very strange and became more and more agitated as we waited for the programme to begin. It was like there was a pressure cooker in my body. Then suddenly, I couldn't breathe; I felt pain in my chest and down my arm and the blood was pumping in my head. Something was very wrong. I couldn't get my words out. I slid from my chair onto the floor.

My parents and Jemma were terrified and phoned an ambulance to get me to hospital as quickly as possible. They recognised I was having some kind of attack and knew they had to act immediately. I was taken to the Princess of Wales Hospital in Bridgend to have all sorts of tests and the conclusion, at the time, was that I was completely exhausted and had suffered some kind of stroke. I was unable to exercise for six months and told that I needed to report to the hospital regularly while they looked into what had caused the attack.

I just couldn't take all the pressure anymore and the studio argument had been the final straw – a breaking point for me. The deceit about my personal life was still giving me the most stress of all. Now, though, I had time to think through the dark periods I was going through in my personal life. I hated myself for all the cheating. I could see that my refusal to tell the truth was making other people tell lies, too, since they believed what I was telling them. I was causing chaos because I wasn't being honest to those I loved and to myself. But to tell my wife that I was gay would be horrendous. I would be hurting the person who loved me beyond everything and I loved her too much to hurt her more. I was at my lowest and felt there was no one I could turn to in order to talk about what was happening to me. I only knew that I should be honest to Jemma first and foremost. She deserved the truth from me.

That period was the darkest time in my life. I couldn't lie any longer. I could see what it was doing to me and to those I loved. There seemed only one way out. Suicide seemed to be the solution to my suffering and the pain that I was causing to others. I felt I had reached rock bottom and that I had nothing more to give. I lost hold of reality and sometimes felt I was acting out my life as if I was in a film. I felt unable to continue the life I was living any longer.

In my daily walks along the coastal path, I began to plan the act that I could see was the only thing to remove my pain. I had made my decision. I walked to the edge of the cliff and prepared to jump off, believing this would be best for everyone. All the lies would be over and there would be peace in my head. But, in the end, something pulled me back. Something saved me and made me think again about the awful action I was about to take.

I had to come to terms with who I really was. I realised that I couldn't run away from telling Jemma any longer. My bravery on the pitch had never been in doubt and I had to find that courage now to save her pain. Telling my wife was the hardest moment for me. I had planned to think through everything I wanted to say to her and tell her as gently as I could. But the reality was not like that. In the end I blurted out, 'I'm gay and I don't know how long I can carry on doing this.'

Finally, the truth was out. Jemma was hurt and angry and had every right to be. Her honest response was typical of her. She could see that if our difficulties had been about another woman, we could have fought for our marriage, but my being gay meant she couldn't compete. She had always loved me and I loved her, too, but I had to stop being selfish and ruining her life. I had only ever wanted the best for her. We comforted each other, realising there was no way back from this. She was going to leave me.

Chapter 7

'Alfie is loyal, inspirational and a real leader of men.'
Martyn Williams MBE, Wales and British and Irish Lions

I returned to international rugby in 2006 for a match against Australia at the Millennium Stadium. My usual excitement at being in the iconic headquarters of Welsh rugby was not there. I was a shadow of my former self in body and in spirit. I had lost a stone in weight, there were bags under my eyes and my skin was grey and lifeless. I couldn't motivate myself to feel anything about the game ahead of me. All through the training sessions before the match, I felt people were examining me closely and talking about how awful I looked. I had been replaced as captain by Stephen Jones. The newspapers described it as 'a body blow' for me to lose the captaincy but I was so unwell that I couldn't take in how things were changing.

I was being watched in a stadium filled with seventy thousand fans and none of them knew what was happening to me during the game. Although the crowd shouted 'Come on, Alfie!', neither they nor I knew who the real Alfie was that day. As a sportsman, I had always prided myself on giving one hundred per cent to the game. In this game, though, I had no idea what was going on around me. There is a photo from the game in which I am leaning back, arms behind my head, open-mouthed and unable to focus. It says everything about how I felt inside. The match ended in a draw, 29–29. Everything was falling apart in front of my eyes – my marriage, my game and myself. Something had to be done about it. I had to make a

37

decision beyond rugby. The next decision was to be life-changing.

I walked off the pitch in despair and was in tears in the changing room after the game. The boys withdrew and tried to give me space, thinking the problem was the score and that I felt unhappy with my own performance. Nobody knew what to do and I just sat there blaming myself for everything. Scott Johnson, the coach of the Australian rugby team, who had previously been Wales' assistant coach, came into the changing room and saw me crying silently, unable to control my feelings.

He was a big man, in many ways, and, as he towered over me, he could see what I had been reduced to. He wanted to know what was wrong and his concern was genuine. I instinctively knew that he would not abandon me. I told him that Jemma had left me. He offered me the chance finally to give up my secret. 'Why?' he asked. Time seemed to stand still. This was the moment that I had to be honest. It was make or break time in every way. He said that he thought he knew why and he looked directly at me as he said it. I knew telling a lie now would be the end for me, so I told him the real reason. That I was gay.

I will never forget what he did then. He told me simply that the team, my team, would always be there for me and would support me. He wanted me to understand that I no longer had to go through this alone. He made me pull myself together that day and he took control of supporting me. He spoke to two of the most senior players, Martyn Williams and Stephen Jones, the now injured captain, and asked them to meet him in the bar. He told them, without fuss, what was happening to me and I really believe that he saved my life that day.

I waited for what seemed like an eternity for the players to come back to see me. I had no idea how they would react to the news. What would they think of me? Would they be appalled by what they heard? How could I face them after all the lies? As it turned out, I needn't have worried. Both were supportive, clearly thinking only of me and of my welfare. Their simple and honest responses made me ashamed that I had ever doubted what they would think of me. They each made it clear that our friendship was the same. There was no fuss because there was no need. Nothing had changed. I felt all the stress and strain lift from me. I had no need to lie any longer. They were still the same people I trained with and I was the same person, too.

I had to tell my parents next. I was sick with worry as I drove to their home. For me, the worst part was not telling them that I was gay, but telling them that I had been lying to them for so long. We were a very close family, and so to deny them the truth seemed terrible. Again, there was no need to worry. My father's reaction was, 'So what?' They both made it clear that they would always be there for me, as would my brothers. I should never have expected anything other than that from them. When I told my best mate, Ian (Compo) Greenslade, he just answered quietly, 'I know.' I had felt for so long that I would never be ready to face the world, but suddenly the reactions of those who meant everything to me proved that I could do this. I was finally ready. There would be no more untruths, no more scurrying around, and no more being afraid. This was me – I am gay.

All those who were really important to me had been told and the world hadn't fallen apart. It was for me to start taking back control. I had faced the fear. All that had terrified me and all that I had agonised over for so long hadn't destroyed me. I had gone through so many emotions to get to this point. Now I could begin to start feeling better, stronger and to start living again. I took small steps, but each one took me further and further back towards finding myself.

There were lots of rumours by now and the journalists circled, ready to break whatever story they could find. They continued to try to discover any scrap of gossip about me and hoped to get a photograph that would give them the scoop they craved. They hovered at my house and outside training grounds, waiting to pounce at every opportunity and I was disgusted by the methods they used to try to trap me.

When Jemma moved out, the situation got worse. There were rumours that the journalists had a story and I was warned that I would be outed. But nothing happened. Once again, the rugby team 'family' closed ranks and supported me. Six months later, after the World Cup, I decided to take control and tell my own story. As my true self, I could be angry. The bullied victim was gone and I was no longer prepared to live in fear. I contacted the *Daily Mai*l to give them an interview telling the truth about who I was.

In December 2009 the story came out in the press. On the same day, Cardiff played Toulouse, my former club, out in France. I knew the place would be full of passion as the fans waited for the battle to start on the pitch. Emotions would be high and I wondered what kind of reception I might have to face. We arrived at the changing room, ready to wear our away strip – it was pink! Martyn Williams broke the ice by pointing out loudly that it must be in my honour! We all cracked up – finally we could relax together.

I was worried that facing the French supporters would be very different. I felt sick with nerves but knew I had to go out with my head held high. How would they react? Would there be name-calling? I had to expect abuse from a highly charged crowd, excited by a game that was so crucial to both teams. I knew only too well from my time at Toulouse that the opposition, the 'enemy', would be left in no doubt of what they were facing by the home fans.

There was nowhere to hide. One by one, our names were announced over the tannoy as the team sheet was read out. I anticipated the worst possible reaction, but as 'Gareth Thomas' was called out, both sets of supporters cheered as loudly as each other. I held my breath, unable for a second to understand what had just happened. All of my fears had been proved wrong. I had been welcomed just like everyone else. We lost the match, but I had won yet another small battle. Once again, the game of rugby and all that it stood for did not let me down.

Chapter 8

'The man who single-handedly enhanced the rugby league vocabulary with his alarmingly disarming greeting, "All right, butt!"'

Russell Isaac, documentary maker and rugby broadcaster

Not every response to my coming out as a gay man was positive but that's life and I knew to expect it. I have learned as I look back that everyone has an opinion and it's no good worrying about what people say. I was sure there would be gossip and I wanted to protect my family from that. For Mum and Dad and my brothers, things were no different; they supported me exactly as they always had. They assured me that from now on things could only get better and better. Once again, I thought how lucky I was to have my family. I felt a new-found freedom and a desire to move on in life now that everything was out in the open. The fear of something can be far worse than the reality and I knew now that being open was the only way forward for me. As a sportsman, I was used to being judged on what I did and I needed to be liked and thought well of. Now, for the first time, I was prepared to be judged as myself. I said to myself, 'Take me or leave me, but let me be true to myself. That's all I can ask for.'

I continued my rugby career, refusing to give in to the niggling worries in my head that warned me I was really under the spotlight now. So what? I vowed to train harder and held my head high, determined to prove I was still the same man. The team carried on around me. It was business as usual. The banter continued; the sarcasm if I missed a tackle was no less. The rugby crowds treated me as one of their own to be applauded or shouted at, depending on how I played. That was fair and that was how it should be. I just wanted to be treated the same way as everyone else on the pitch.

I was approached by the media to tell my story in more detail but I was careful about how I wanted this to be portrayed. I was clear that I was first and foremost a man. I was a good son and brother (so they told me!), a good rugby player, a good friend I hoped. What I did not want was to be judged by my sexuality. I was the same person I always had been – the only difference was that now I was honest and open, in my own mind and in the eyes of the world, about who I was.

I was invited to appear on numerous chat shows, to attend celebrity parties and to socialise with people I had only read about in magazines. I turned lots of invitations down. It all sounded good, but I knew straight away that this life wasn't for me. I didn't want to be seen as a symbol.

Importantly, too, I didn't want the actions of those who had been courageous before me to be made less in any way. I was humbled by the responses of people who wrote or stopped me to thank me for what I had done. They shared their stories, their hopes and their fears with me. I cannot say how honoured I felt to be allowed to share their feelings. They often wanted to assure me of the positive support I had from them, and that meant the world to me. They knew what I had gone through as they had been through it too. I had carried a secret for a long time and then learned that others felt just like me – scared, on edge, waiting to be caught out. I could only tell them that life was now starting for me because I had opened up.

I needed to decide what to do next in my playing career. I decided to take on something very different. My next move was to sign up to play rugby league, one of the hardest sports on earth. Family and friends were astonished. 'Why?' they asked. The honest answer was that I had always wanted to play rugby league and this was to be my last challenge as age was against me playing for much longer in professional sport. But this choice certainly was a challenge – in many ways!

I joined the Crusaders in Wrexham, north Wales, in 2010. However, it was not the best of starts as on my debut in March, against Catalans Dragons, live on Sky TV, I was concussed seconds into the match and had to leave the field after thirty minutes. I had felt the full force of sixteen and a half stones of Jamal Fakir, a substantial second row player. I should have come straight off but had to prove to the fans that I was hard enough for the sport. We won the game but I can't say I played a great part in it, looking on dazed from the bench. Both my self-esteem and my body took a blow.

Things got better after that, though. I listened to the coach's advice and trained hard, determined to give my all as I had in rugby union. The team appreciated this. I scored my first try in rugby league against Wakefield Trinity and felt that I had started to make a positive contribution in my new sport.

Not all was positive, though. In one game, against Castleford Tigers, I heard from the crowd a vile chant that took me back briefly to my deepest fears. I felt sick as the words registered and I tried to block out the horror of knowing that this abuse, directed solely at me, could be heard by everyone. Bullies know how to hurt and hide behind group strength. I felt I was alone on the pitch, being baited by a cruel gang. I forced myself to play on but it seemed their words became louder and louder, and I was incapable of blocking them out. Other sections of the crowd tried to shout them down and support me, but I was unable to focus on that, only tuning in to the nasty taunts. They could sense my hurt and were enjoying it, but I could not let them defeat me. I carried on playing, waiting for the end of the game to release me from the torture. We lost the match and I felt that I lost something of myself that day.

Back in the changing room, my teammates were disgusted by what they had witnessed and, once again, the team made me realise how strong the bonds of sport can be. Like Martyn Williams and Stephen Jones earlier, they made no great fuss. They showed by their actions that they were with me and together we were a strong team. There was no need for heated discussion about the rights and wrongs of what had taken place out there. Even players from the Tigers came to apologise and acknowledge the cowardice of one group of their own supporters. It was shocking to those who had witnessed the effect it had. It hurt because I had gone so far to be honest as the first openly gay professional player and now I felt dragged back to a dark place of fear and upset. Luckily, it didn't last, though.

Instead, I became angry and was determined to fight back against the bullies. They could not and would not defeat me. Someone, not me, reported the incident to the Rugby Football League and I had to explain how I felt about the incident. They, like those who had reported the incident, wanted to see proper standards at a game upheld. The easy thing for me would have been to let the matter go, but I felt I had to be honest and supportive and say how it had really affected me. To fail to admit this would have been letting the bullies win. I had to point out to people how unacceptable it was, and how to ignore those unacceptable taunts would mean hurt for others who also tried to be honest. It was another hurdle to get over but one worth fighting for.

To be given the chance to play again for Wales was the ultimate dream for me. On my rugby league international debut against Italy, I was also appointed captain in place of the injured Lee Briers. I felt so proud to be given the opportunity and honour to represent and lead my country again. I managed to score a try in that first game as a rugby league international but sadly we lost the match. The number of supporters that day did not quite match up to those who regularly filled the Millennium Stadium but the glory of playing for Wales, albeit in a different code, was just as great.

We won the European Cup Trophy but my injuries were becoming more frequent and, in 2011, I had to admit that it was time to retire after having missed most of the season. I recognised that I would not make the 2011 rugby league Four Nations tournament. It was impossible for me to give less than my very best for the team and in such a tough sport my body could no longer recover from injuries quickly. I'm glad that I didn't realise when my final game would be as it would have been too painful and difficult for me to face up to that.

Chapter 9

'I admire you. I think you're amazing!'
Ellen Degeneres, American comedian, television host, actress, writer and television producer

Retirement from sport has brought me lots of new and exciting challenges. I worried that I might suddenly have nothing to do and the thought of that was scary. So I decided that I wanted to make a difference, to use my 'celebrity' status in a positive way, to encourage openness and freedom from fear for others. I understood how easy it was to allow your inner fears to block out hope and to be afraid to take new opportunities. I wanted my story to give others the strength to pursue their lives and their dreams openly. I knew only too well about the voice inside that tells you to hide and I wanted to give others support in being kind to themselves and not to feel threatened and persecuted. This was how I could pay back the kindness and care of others who had been there for me.

Even though I had given up playing, I was given the opportunity to be part of ITV's Rugby World Cup coverage in 2011, which I really enjoyed. It gave me the chance to look at the game in a totally different light. I wasn't breaking sweat on the pitch, but at first this was far more terrifying to me. I had to learn to follow signals from the studio and be ready to provide explanations and opinions on the spot. I was a pundit along with Sean Fitzpatrick, Michael Lynagh, François Pienaar, Lawrence Dallaglio and Thom Evans. ITV tried hard to provide a balance of ex-players and nationalities and it certainly got us talking! Everyone found it amusing that I was described as 'window dressing' in an online forum – I had to laugh too!

I was also invited to Los Angeles to appear on the 'Ellen Degeneres Show'. Ellen is a pioneer gay comedian and talk-show host and is extremely successful and well known. I was in awe of being included on a show that ran for five days a week on prime-time American television, with guests from the best of American TV, film and music. I was billed as 'The inspiring Gareth Thomas shares his story'. I still found it hard to understand and take in how positively people responded to me and was humbled by their care and support.

Ellen appreciated from her own perspective how hard it was for gay people to come out, and generously praised me for doing so in a traditionally 'hard' and macho sportsman's world. I talked to her audience about how I had become the master of playing the straight man, always being the first to the bar, drinking the most and starting fights to prove my masculinity. She listened carefully and sympathetically as I told her that I had prayed to be straight. She and the audience cheered loudly as I told her the story of my dad, a down-to-earth man not given to shows of emotion, bringing in champagne to toast the start of my new life as an openly gay man. He still loves that Ellen said on TV, 'What a cool dad!' and reminds me of it. I counter by telling him that she said I was amazing!

The following year offered more new experiences for me. I was contacted by the world-famous French shoe designer Christian Louboutin, known for his signature red soles. At first I couldn't believe it! His shoes were very expensive and worn by stars like Victoria Beckham and Jennifer Lopez, who sang about his 'sexy heels'. His first customer had been Princess Caroline of Monaco, so I was certainly different! He sent me a pair of custom-made slip-ons, embroidered with replicas of my tattoos – a far cry from my early trainers from Woolworths! We did a photo shoot together dressed in matching white rugby kit and got on tremendously. I even took him back to Bridgend to sample my mum's cheese baguettes – not real French cuisine but definitely enjoyed by him! She loves to tell that story at every opportunity.

In 2012, I also accepted the chance to enter the Celebrity Big Brother house, aware that I was doing something well outside my comfort zone again. I realised that the only way to do it and survive was to be myself in there. I wanted people to get to know me away from the rugby pitch or sports pages. I understood the danger of being on television in a reality show but I also knew it gave the public the chance to see who I really was. I was very nervous going into the house, especially as I was touted originally as the bookies' favourite. Others may have looked for fame or excitement in the eight previous series of the show, but I just wanted to get on with the other housemates and not be evicted too soon! I became good friends with Nicola McLean, the glamour model, and chatted to everyone as I always did. Housemates like Natalie Cassidy and Denise Welch, who eventually won, understood how television worked and helped me avoid any obvious pitfalls. I came third and was genuinely surprised to get so far. Far more important to me were the lovely tributes given by my fellow housemates – I felt part of a team again.

In 2013, I became part of a team of two: my ice-skating partner Robin Johnstone and myself. I agreed to take part in ITV's *Dancing on Ice*, an amazing challenge considering my shape and muscles! I never thought in a million years that I would grow to love it as I did. Training was hard but for the entire six months Robin was patient and spent time making sure I built up my confidence. This was again so different for me. I had to learn how to project a personality and how to act out a role, something that was certainly not part of the sport I was used to. Also, I had to learn to dance, something I had always struggled with. I learned so much from the great Jayne Torvill and Christopher Dean who were the mentors and experts on the show. Imagine being given lessons by world champions, the best in the ice-dance business! All the competitors looked on enviously when they skated effortlessly and gracefully around the rink. My efforts were not quite the same…

I did, however, manage to make it to the semi-final, but was withdrawn from the final by the show's doctors, on grounds of ill health. After examining me during training, they ruled that I was too ill to continue, because I couldn't stop vomiting each time I tried to stand. I kept fainting and I suffered from memory loss, which was very strange. It turned out I had become extremely ill with motion sickness after a difficult flying routine and there was no way that they would let me return. Phillip Schofield announced my withdrawal and Twitter was deluged with messages of goodwill, which was amazing. Everyone was genuinely disappointed for me, and all the other competitors sympathised with what had happened to me. I was really upset to have to pull out of the competition. I am not a quitter and I tried my hardest to keep going, but people were concerned that I might suffer another mini stroke if I continued to put my body under pressure. So my television ice-dance career ended before the final.

Television chat shows also began to contact me. Appearing on ITV's *Loose Women* filled me with more fear than facing any rugby team! I needn't have worried though. Everyone was lovely and put me at ease, and the positive Facebook comments after the programme made a huge difference to my confidence. I also appeared on Jonathan Ross's show. He introduced me as a superstar from the world of rugby, saying that he felt that speaking about my personal life had been even more impressive than my contribution on the field.

Jonathan and I made such a connection that when I spoke to him about what I had gone through it felt like there were only the two of us in the room. He was a very special interviewer who really listened to my answers. I trusted him and forgot completely that I was on television. I was moved to tears by Jonathan's final words as I knew how much they meant to him. He said, 'One of my children is gay and I understand the impact when someone like you stands up... I want to thank you personally for what you are doing.'

Much has been said about Mickey Rourke, the Hollywood legend, and his desire to star in a film about my story. It was a huge honour for me to meet him. The Oscar-nominated actor wanted to know more about how and why I had kept my secret for such a long time. Who knows if it will happen but I'd like to see it! He has said it will be ten times better than his epic film *The Wrestler*, so watch this space…

I was also thrilled to be given a cameo role as myself in the comedy drama *Stella*, set in the Welsh valleys. It is one of my favourite television programmes and I couldn't wait to be a part of it. There was a lot of hanging around on set but I loved every second. The cast and crew made me feel very welcome. My very small acting part was to shake someone's hand at Dai Dropkick's funeral. I was there for a whole day filming and when the episode was broadcast I gathered all the family together to see my great acting role. Sadly, I was on screen for less than a second!

I didn't give up on acting though – I was thrilled to be chosen to play Dandini in 'Cinderella' at Christmas in Cardiff. I loved it! Panto is all about not taking yourself too seriously and, for me, life had been serious for too long. Now I could go on stage and enjoy others laughing at me and be able to laugh at myself. It was six weeks of pure fun and enjoyment. The cast was brilliant and we became like family – another great team! Everyone worked hard and played hard too. When we weren't on stage we shared jokes and secrets and I made lifelong friends.

I am also the subject of a play, *Crouch, Touch, Pause, Engage*. I am working alongside young people from Bridgend and two theatre companies, Out of Joint and the National Theatre Wales. The play centres on sport, politics, secrets and, crucially for me, the need to learn to be yourself. The play is summed up with: 'This is the story of two Welsh names bruised, but not beaten, by media speculation: Gareth "Alfie" Thomas, 100 caps for Wales, once its captain, now the world's most prominent gay sportsman; and his hometown, Bridgend.'

My book, *Proud*, written with Michael Calvin, a sportswriter with the *Independent on Sunday* is very important to me. The title was chosen to describe me as a gay man, a rugby man, but above all as a man, a human being. The title sums up how I now feel. I am, indeed, proud of what I have achieved. Writing it, going over difficult times in my life, was hard, but it represents my journey, and if it can help others that is all I could ask for. Some say I have been brave putting it out for the world to read. I just know that it represents the next stage in my life and I want to live that life as openly and honestly as I wish for others.

Chapter 10

*'It's not **what** you want to be but **who** you want to be'*
Gareth Thomas

Supporting Childline has always been something very close to my heart. Emanuele Palladino, my good friend and business manager, knew of my desire to get involved with the organisation and help in any way I could. His wife worked for Childline and I respected all of their great work carried out to help young people. They were looking for a role model to talk about issues of homosexuality and, bearing in mind everything that I had gone through, I knew straight away that this would really be worthwhile and not just a project I lent my name to. I wanted to talk from my personal viewpoint and understanding about the campaign's message, 'Be yourself rather than what society expects you to be'. It took me a lot of heartache to understand what this meant and I wanted to help others to see this a lot sooner than I had.

I decided to work in organisations across the country, talking about identifying bullying and suggesting ways to cope and to find the courage to defeat it. I am proud of my work with Stonewall in raising the profile of their campaign, 'Education for all', tackling homophobic bullying in schools. I was named their 'Hero of the Year' in 2010, but I always say I accepted the award on behalf of the real heroes, the silent people who carry on battling.

I am backing a schools' campaign, 'Balls to Bullying', because I want young people to understand that everyone is vulnerable to being bullied, no matter how tough they may seem. In this role, I give talks where I work through possible scenarios that might occur in schools or colleges and offer advice on finding support. The feedback has been very positive and I hope that people will be able to use my suggestions to feel stronger and find ways to tackle their problems. No matter how old you are, it is easy to let fear take control.

I find that encouraging people to talk, and to realise that everyone has worries, makes their own problems seem more manageable and less terrifying. The pupils often seem shocked that a strong, fit rugby player, and particularly an ex-captain of the Wales rugby team, can admit to feeling isolated and in fear. They talk to me about how they feel weak and ashamed that they can't stand up for themselves.

I want people to learn that it is the bullies who are weak and, if I can get that message across and help in any way, I will have achieved my mission. I have received so many letters from people who pour their feelings out, seeing in my story something that they can recognise. Sometimes, people come up to me just to whisper, 'Thank you'. They say that I have given them the strength to take the first step. This means more to me than all the caps, cups and trophies I have won in my career.

I decided that I would not be bullied by the 'red tops', those newspapers who threatened to tell my story to the world, but that I would tell it myself on my own terms. I had no idea what people's reactions would be. I was the first person in professional rugby to come out. I'm not ashamed to say I was petrified about how people would behave towards me. I became stronger, though, because *I* made the decision. I didn't come out in order to be the first gay player in the game. I came out to start living my life openly. I made the choice not to shrivel up inside but to start living and enjoying life. And I have huge admiration for others who have done so in the world of sport. People like Tom Daley and John Amaechi, I salute you.

It is wonderful for me now to be honest and open, both in words and actions. My partner Ian and I are now happy to live our life together as we want to and as it should be.

It takes courage to be who you are, but it is worth it.

Quick Reads 2015

My Sporting Heroes – Jason Mohammad
Captain Courage – Gareth Thomas
Code Black: Winter of Storm Surfing – Tom
Anderson
Cwtch Me if You Can – Beth Reekles

For more information about **Quick Reads**

and other **Accent Press** titles

please visit

www.accentpress.co.uk